Benjamin Franklin

from A to Z

If you would not be forgotten as soon as
you are dead,
Either write something worth reading,
or do something
Worth writing.

Benjamin Franklin from A to Z

By Laura Crawford

Illustrated by Judith Hierstein

PELICAN PUBLISHING COMPANY
Gretna 2013

To the students and teachers of Sleepy Hollow Elementary School. You inspire me every day!—LC

The word "Pelican" and the depiction of a pelican are trademarks of Pelican Publishing Company, Inc., and are registered in the U.S. Patent and Trademark Office.

Library of Congress Cataloging-in-Publication Data

Crawford, Laura.
  Benjamin Franklin from A to Z / by Laura Crawford ; illustrated by Judith Hierstein.
    p. cm.
  ISBN 978-1-4556-1713-5 (hardcover : alk. paper)—ISBN 978-1-4556-1714-2 (e-book) 1. Franklin, Benjamin, 1706-1790—Juvenile literature. 2. Statesmen—United States—Biography—Juvenile literature. 3. Scientists—United States—Biography—Juvenile literature. 4. Inventors—United States—Biography—Juvenile literature. 5. Printers—United States—Biography—Juvenile literature. 6. Alphabet books—Juvenile literature. I. Hierstein, Judy, ill. II. Title.
  E302.6.F8C7825 2013
  973.3092—dc23
  [B]

                    2012016169

Printed in Malaysia
Published by Pelican Publishing Company, Inc.
1000 Burmaster Street, Gretna, Louisiana 70053

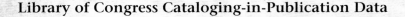

A is for American hero

Benjamin Franklin was a very important person in our country's history. He was a printer, author, inventor, musician, scientist, and politician. One of his greatest accomplishments was helping to form a new country called the United States of America.

B *is for Boston*

Benjamin was born in Boston, Massachusetts, on January 17, 1706, and was the fifteenth of seventeen children. His parents wanted him to become a minister, but they didn't have enough money to keep him in school. With only two years of formal education, he continued learning through constant reading.

C is for the Second Continental Congress

In May of 1775, delegates from the thirteen colonies came together in Philadelphia, Pennsylvania, to form the Second Continental Congress. Franklin and fifty-five other representatives made many decisions about how this new country would work. As a result of this meeting, an army was formed with George Washington as the commander.

D is for Declaration of Independence

In May of 1775, the Second Continental Congress gave Benjamin Franklin, Thomas Jefferson, John Adams, Robert Livingston, and Roger Sherman a job. They were to create a document stating that the colonies wanted their freedom from England. Jefferson wrote the first draft of the Declaration of Independence, and Franklin and the others helped him make minor changes.

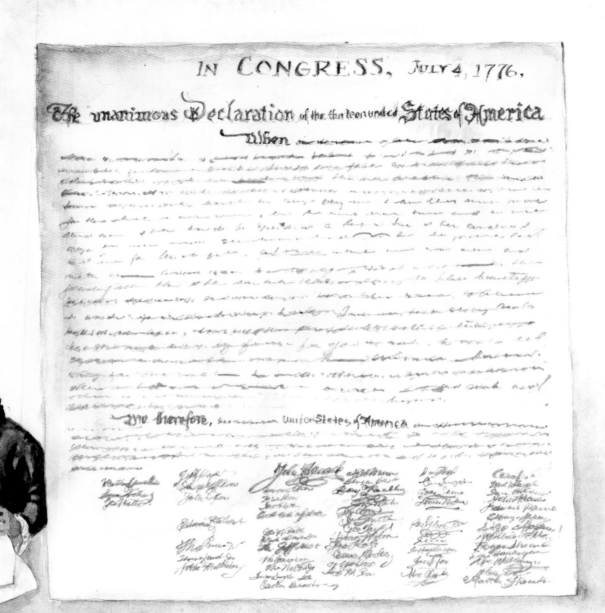

E is for equality

Fifty-six delegates signed the Declaration of Independence. It states "that all men are created equal, that they are endowed by their Creator with certain unalienable Rights, that among these are Life, Liberty and the pursuit of Happiness." Working on this document was one of Franklin's greatest contributions to the world.

F is for fire department

In 1736, Franklin organized a group of volunteers to form the first fire department in Philadelphia. They used leather buckets to carry water and protect their belongings. About thirteen years later, he invented the lightning rod, a metal pole placed on top of a tall building that attracted lightning and carried it into the ground. This prevented houses from catching on fire.

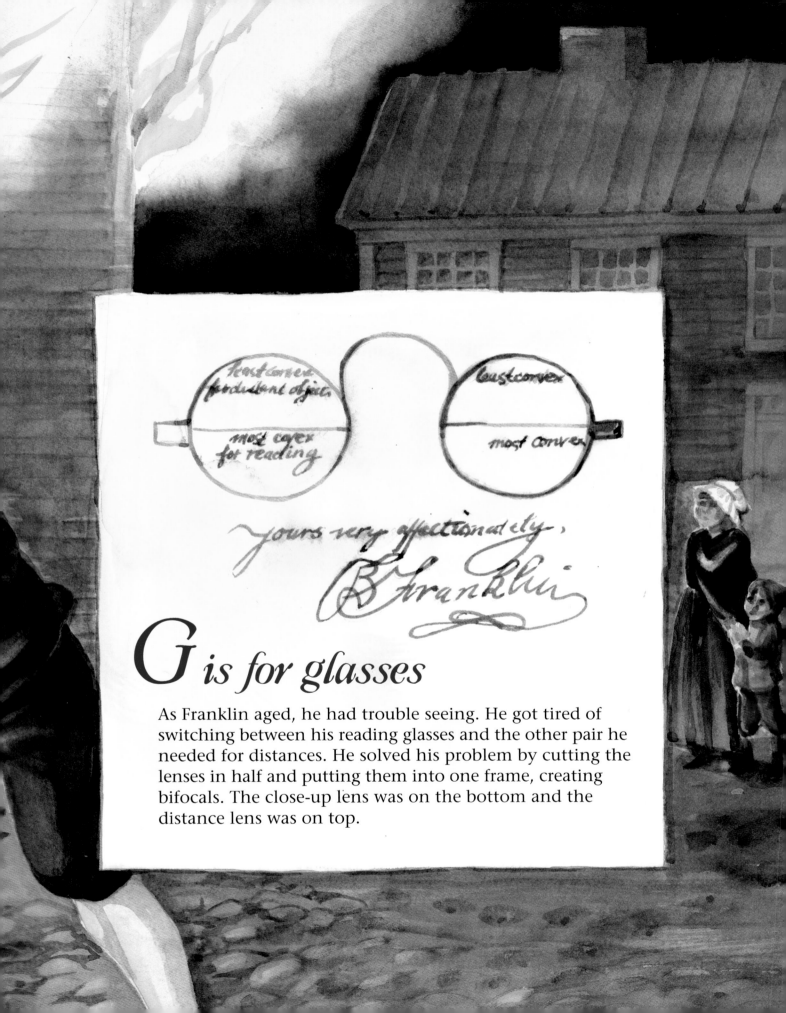

G is for glasses

As Franklin aged, he had trouble seeing. He got tired of switching between his reading glasses and the other pair he needed for distances. He solved his problem by cutting the lenses in half and putting them into one frame, creating bifocals. The close-up lens was on the bottom and the distance lens was on top.

H is for hospital

Franklin and Dr. Thomas Bond started the nation's first hospital in 1751. It was Dr. Bond's idea, but he didn't have enough money. Franklin helped raise funds, and the two friends founded Pennsylvania Hospital. Their goal was "to care for the sick-poor and insane who were wandering the streets of Philadelphia."

I is for iron stove

In the 1700s, most people warmed their homes with wood-burning fireplaces. Franklin designed an iron stove called the Pennsylvania Fireplace that used less wood and was much safer. It also produced more heat and less smoke. Today it's called the Franklin Stove.

J is for July 1776

The fourth of July is considered the birthday of the United States of America. On this date in 1776, the Continental Congress approved the Declaration of Independence. On July 8, the Liberty Bell was rung, calling people together to the Pennsylvania State House where the document was read out loud.

K is for kite experiment

In 1752, Benjamin and his son William conducted an experiment. They stood in a thunderstorm holding a silk kite with a key tied to the string. When lightning hit the kite, the electric current traveled through the kite and the string, proving that lightning and electricity were the same!

L *is for library*

In the 1720s, Franklin and twelve men formed a club called the Junto. They met on Friday nights to discuss politics and share books. This gave them an idea; they would start a lending library on a larger scale. They each donated part of their collection and forty shillings and paid annual dues to collectively buy books. This was the beginning of the Library Company of Philadelphia.

A Magic Square of Squares.

52	61	4	13	20	29	36	45
14	3	62	51	46	35	30	19
53	60	5	12	21	28	37	44
11	6	59	54	43	38	27	22
55	58	7	10	23	26	39	42
9	8	57	56	41	40	25	24
50	63	2	15	18	31	34	47
16	1	64	49	48	33	32	17

M is for magic square

One day, when Franklin was tired of listening to a political debate, he started doing math problems. He created a "magic square," a grid with sixty-four numbers. He became fascinated with the number patterns and figured out an arrangement so that, when added horizontally, vertically, or diagonally, the sum was always 260!

N is for night watch

Franklin wanted Philadelphia to be peaceful, safe, and clean. He advocated for a night watch group to patrol the city. He suggested other city improvements too. After seeing a woman sweeping the dusty roads, Benjamin wanted the streets to be paved. He also found that rounded oil lamps became dirty quickly, and the streets were then too dark. He solved the problem by designing lamps with four glass panes and a tube that allowed the smoke to escape.

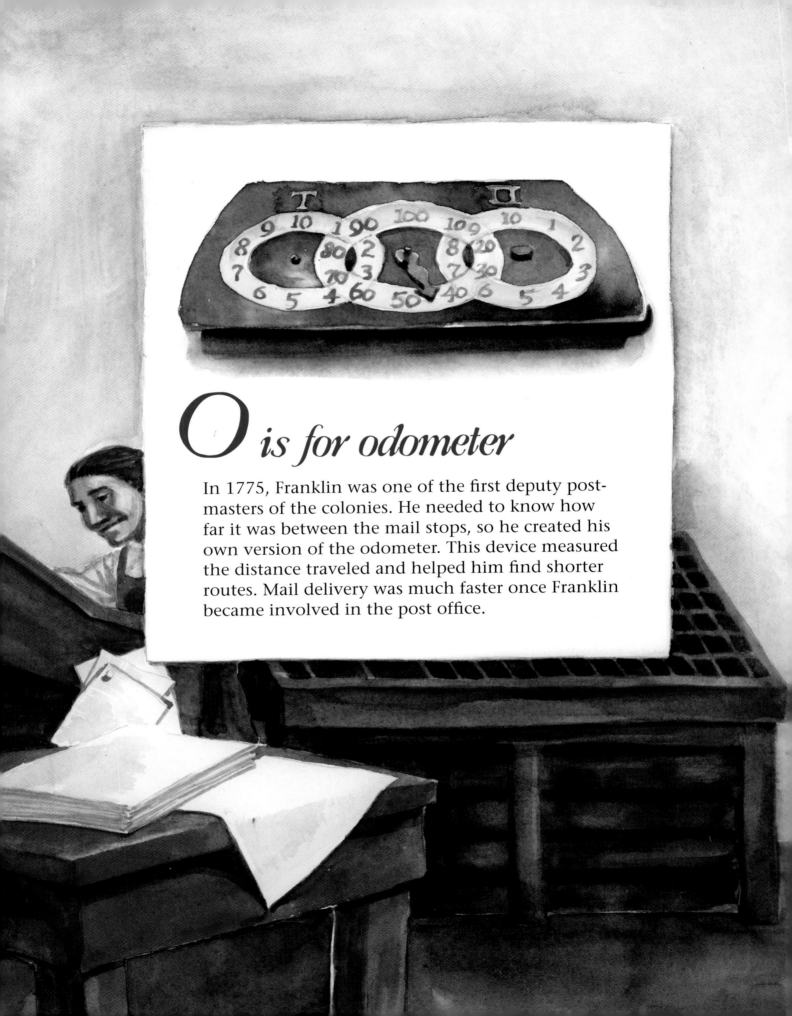

O *is for odometer*

In 1775, Franklin was one of the first deputy postmasters of the colonies. He needed to know how far it was between the mail stops, so he created his own version of the odometer. This device measured the distance traveled and helped him find shorter routes. Mail delivery was much faster once Franklin became involved in the post office.

P is for printer

Reading, writing, and printing were a huge part of Franklin's life. When he was twelve, he worked as an apprentice at his brother James' printing shop. He learned the trade and secretly wrote articles for his brother's newspaper. As an adult, he printed the *Pennsylvania Gazette*, a newspaper which published news stories, cartoons, and pictures. He wanted people who couldn't read to learn from his paper, too.

Q is for quotations

Franklin wrote *Poor Richard's Almanack*, a popular book which was published for twenty-five years. He was always thinking of ways to be a better person and wanted to help others do the same. The almanac had quotations such as "An apple a day keeps the doctor away," and "Honesty is the best policy." The almanac also included weather forecasts, jokes, riddles, and poems. Because most people did not have many books, he wanted his book to be both useful and entertaining.

R *is for respect*

Franklin was one of the most respected men in our history. He was a Founding Father and one of the older politicians of the time. Franklin's fame in France was due to his experiments and inventions. He was invited to fancy parties and had many admirers. When Franklin died in 1790 in Philadelphia, more than 20,000 people watched his funeral procession.

S is for swimming

Franklin loved to swim and is even in the International Swimming Hall of Fame! When he was young, he taught himself how to swim after reading a book. When Benjamin was eleven, he wanted to swim faster, so he made flippers for his hands. He also discovered that if he flew a kite on a windy day, he would be pulled across the lake by holding onto the string!

T is for turkey

The bald eagle is a symbol of the United States. Franklin didn't agree with this choice; he wanted the turkey to be the national bird. In a letter to his daughter, Sally, he said the bald eagle "is a bird of bad moral character" and a turkey "is much more respectable."

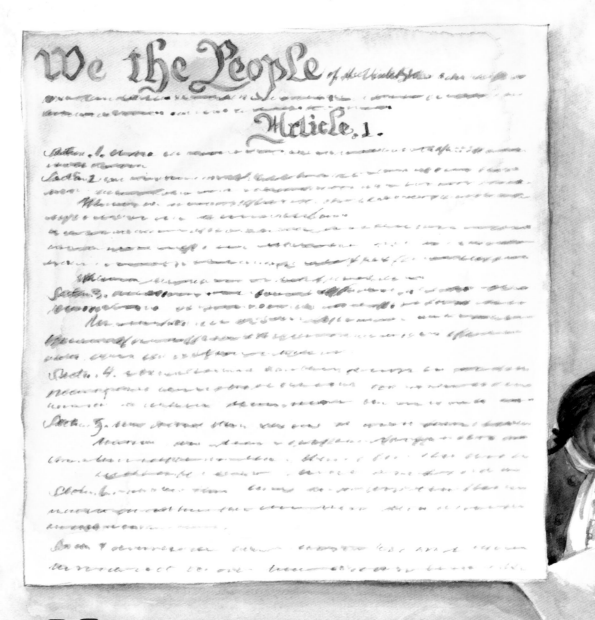

U is for United States Constitution

When he was eighty-one years old, Franklin and the other delegates from the states came together to form the Constitutional Convention. Many of the men disagreed about how to organize the government, but Franklin gave a persuasive speech. Most supported the new government plan. In the end, thirty-nine of the fifty-five delegates signed the United States Constitution in 1787.

V is for victory

Franklin, John Adams, and John Jay represented the new country and signed the Treaty of Paris in 1783. This agreement formally ended the Revolutionary War, and England recognized the United States as a nation. It also stated that England would remove its troops. The small army of colonists had been victorious over the English army.

W is for William

William was Benjamin's oldest son. He and his father were close but disagreed when it came to the Revolutionary War. Ben worked for the colonies' independence, and William remained loyal to England. Ben said, "Nothing has ever hurt me so much . . . as to find myself deserted in my old age by my only son."

X is... gone!

There was not an X in Franklin's phonetic alphabet! While living in England, he wrote *A Scheme for a New Alphabet*. He was fascinated by letters and sounds but thought they were confusing. He said some letters were unnecessary because they made similar sounds, so he took out the letters *c, q, w, x,* and *y*.

Y is for yellow fever

In the 1700s, Franklin worried about yellow fever, a dangerous disease that killed many people and often spread through water. In his will, he left Boston and Philadelphia a large sum of money to fix their water systems and hopefully prevent the spread of yellow fever.

Z is for zeal

Another word for zeal is passion. Benjamin Franklin had zeal for everything he did: inventing, writing, volunteering, and improving his country. Ben could have become rich from his inventions, but he did not. He believed that others should benefit from his inventions, and new ideas should be shared. People all over the world use his creations every day!

The Life and Times of Benjamin Franklin

1706 . . . . . Born in Boston, Massachusetts, on January 17

1714 . . . . . Studies at a Boston grammar school

1717 . . . . . Invents swimming fins

1718 . . . . . Begins an apprenticeship in James' printing shop in Boston

1723 . . . . . Leaves for Philadelphia, Pennsylvania

1724 . . . . Moves to London, continuing his training as a printer

1726 . . . . . Returns to Philadelphia

1727 . . . . . Begins the Junto

1728 . . . . . Opens his printing office in Philadelphia

1729 . . . . . Becomes sole owner and publisher of the *Pennsylvania Gazette*

1731 . . . . . Son William is born; Starts the Library Company of Philadelphia

1732 . . . . . Youngest son Francis is born

1732-58 . Publishes *Poor Richard: An Almanack*

1736 . . . . . Son Francis dies; Starts the Union Fire Company in Philadelphia

1737 . . . . . Is appointed postmaster of Philadelphia

1741 . . . . . Designs Franklin Stove

1743 . . . . . Daughter Sarah is born

1747 . . . . . First writes of electrical experimentation; Organizes the first militia

1748 . . . . . Sells printing office and retires from business

(continued on next page)

The Life and Times of Benjamin Franklin

1750 . . . . . Proposes lightening rod

1752 . . . . . Performs famous kite experiment; Philadelphia Hospital opens

1756 . . . . . Invents new kind of street lamp

1757 . . . . . Sails to England

1757-62 . . Travels to England and serves as a representative of the Pennsylvania Assembly

1764 . . . . . Sails to London

1767 . . . . . Sails to France

1774 . . . . . Wife Deborah dies while Ben is in Europe

1775 . . . . . Returns to Philadelphia; Elected to Second Continental Congress; Elected postmaster of the colonies; Creates an odometer to improve mail delivery

1776 . . . . . Signs the Declaration of Independence; Sails to France

1782-83 . . The Treaty of Paris is negotiated and ratified, officially ending the American Revolution; Invents bifocal lenses

1784 . . . . . Proposes the turkey as the symbol of the United States

1785 . . . . . Returns to Philadelphia

1787 . . . . . Serves as a delegate to the Constitutional Convention; Helps write the Constitution of the United States

1790 . . . . . At age eighty-four, Benjamin Franklin dies in Philadelphia